Patterns in Nature

by Maria Alaina

Wonder Readers are published by Capstone Press,
1710 Roe Crest Drive, North Mankato, Minnesota 56003.
www.capstonepub.com

Library of Congress Cataloging-in-Publication Data
Alaina, Maria.
  Patterns in nature / Maria Alaina. — 1st ed.
    p. cm. — (Wonder readers)
  Includes index.
  ISBN 978-1-4765-0034-8 (library binding)
  ISBN 978-1-4296-7815-5 (paperback)
  ISBN 978-1-4765-0847-4 (eBook PDF)
  1. Sequences (Mathematics)—Juvenile literature. 2. Pattern perception—Juvenile literature. I. Title.
  QA292.A426 2013
  508—dc23   2011023076

Summary: "Describes a variety of patterns found in the natural world"—Provided by publisher.

Editorial Credits

Maryellen Gregoire, project director; Mary Lindeen, consulting editor; Gene Bentdahl, designer;
Sarah Schuette, editor; Wanda Winch, media researcher; Eric Manske, production specialist

Photo Credits

Dreamstime: Anobis, 18 (bottom right); Shutterstock: Audrey Snider-Bell, 12, djgis, 17, FotoVeto, cover,
Galyna Andrushko, 10, Gurgen Bakhshetsyan, 6, hallam creations, 18 (bottom left), Hannamariah, 18 (top
right), Harald Toepfer, 4, Irina Yun, 14, Krasowit, 7, LilKar, 9, Mana Photo, 16, Michael Shake, 8, palko72,
11, Patricia Hofmeester, 13, Paul Orr, 18 (top left), Smart-foto, 1, szefei, 5, Willem Dijkstra, 15

Word Count: **163**   Guided Reading Level: **G**   Early Intervention Level: **16**

Printed in China.
092012   006934LEOS13

Table of Contents

Note to Parents and Teachers

The Wonder Readers Next Steps: Math series supports national mathematics standards. These titles use text structures that support early readers, specifically with a close photo/text match and glossary. Each book is perfectly leveled to support the reader at the right reading level, and the topics are of high interest. Early readers will gain success when they are presented with a book that is of interest to them and is written at the appropriate level.

A **pattern** is a set of shapes
or symbols that are **repeated**.
Patterns are found everywhere
in our world.

Plant Patterns

Plants have patterns.

This mushroom has a pattern
on its cap.

Acorns and leaves have patterns.
Look closely at the acorn cap.

Animal Patterns

There are all kinds of animal patterns.
Some animals make patterns.
Many spiders make patterns in webs.

Honeybees make patterns
in honeycomb.

Snakes make patterns in the
sand when they move.

Some animals have patterns on their skin. Zebras have patterns of stripes.

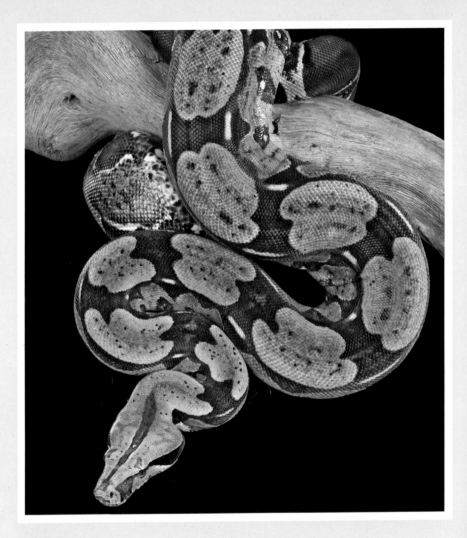

The pattern on this snake's skin
tells what kind of snake it is.

Some feathers have patterns on them.

This shell has a pattern. See how the lines on the shell repeat?

This butterfly has a pattern
on its wings that looks like eyes.

Patterns in Water

This wave has a pattern. There are lines leading to the top of the curving wave.

Raindrops make a pattern on the grass.

Patterns are everywhere in nature!

Now Try This!

Look for patterns in your classroom: on the walls, on the floor, on books, and on clothing. Look for patterns of shape, size, and color. On a sheet of paper, copy the pattern you like best. Then draw your own pattern!

Glossary

acorn   the nut of an oak tree

pattern   a set of shapes, colors, or lines that appear in some order over and over again

repeat   to say, do, or make again

Internet Sites

FactHound offers a safe, fun way to find Internet sites related to this book. All of the sites on FactHound have been researched by our staff.

Here's all you do:

Visit *www.facthound.com*

Type in this code: 9781476500348

 Check out projects, games and lots more at
www.capstonekids.com

Index